LOOKING FOR SHILOH

LOOKING FOR SHILOH

Poems by
Edsel Ford

UNIVERSITY OF MISSOURI PRESS

COLUMBIA • MISSOURI

ACKNOWLEDGMENT

Certain of these poems first appeared elsewhere. For permission to reprint here, grateful acknowledgment is made to the editors and publishers of *The Beloit Poetry Journal, The Delta Review, The Georgia Review, The Kansas City Star, Kansas Magazine, The Literary Review, Mademoiselle, The Massachusetts Review, The Midwest Quarterly, New Mexico Quarterly, New Orleans Review, The New York Herald Tribune, The New York Times, The Ozarks Mountaineer, The Poetry Society of Georgia Yearbook, Poetry Society of Texas Book of the Year, Saturday Review, Shenandoah: The Washington and Lee University Review, South and West, Southwest Review, The Texas Quarterly, United Church Herald, The University Review, Voices,* and *The Wormwood Review.*

"About Grampa, Who Died Poor" was first published in *Mademoiselle;* copyright © by The Condé Nast Publications, Inc.

"On a Warm Winter Day, on a Residential Street" is reprinted from *The Massachusetts Review;* © 1962, The Massachusetts Review, Inc.

"Pecos River" and "Contingent" © 1962/1964 by The New York Times Company. Reprinted by permission.

"Salt" and "Hitch-Hiker" were first published in *Shenandoah: The Washington and Lee University Review.* Reprinted by permission.

"Storm Cellar" and "The Road to Hanoi" were first published in *Southwest Review.* Reprinted by permission.

THE DEVINS MEMORIAL AWARD

A PROVISION of the Devins Memorial Award, the major prize of the Kansas City Poetry Contests, is publication of the winning manuscript by the University of Missouri Press.

Looking for Shiloh, by Edsel Ford, was chosen from over four hundred and fifty manuscripts submitted anonymously by poets throughout the United States.

The Award is made possible by the generosity of Dr. and Mrs. Edward A. Devins. Dr. Devins is former President of the Kansas City Jewish Community Center and is a patron of the Center's American Poets Series.

for Hank

Morning Song

The poet hangs out his socks and the day begins.
The lady next door twitters like a canary
Released from bondage; the elm grows up the sky;
The postman unfreezes from his little cart;
The frog in the pansies brings his tongue back in;
Dogs bark; the garbage thunders in the can;
And songs, like the gentle rain from the heavens, fall.

CONTENTS

I

Tourists at Mid-Moment

. . . I came upon a priest once at St. Andrew's in Amalfi in crimson and gold brocade riding the clouds of his belief.

It happened that we tourists had intervened at some mid-moment of the ritual—tipped the sacristan or whatever it was.

—William Carlos Williams

Looking for Shiloh on a country road
To keep its appointment as the sign had promised,
We forded two streams where, coming out,
The car shed water like a running bird.

What this Shiloh might be, we couldn't guess.
But, crossroads or country church with tongueless bell
And stones leaning over tongueless dust,
It had a poetry about its name.

Pursuing Shiloh like a rhyme for silver,
We clung to the clay road cutting through the woodland
Till the sudden sight of two immobile crows
Trounced on the brake, and I reversed the car.

"*Decoys,*" you said, and I in my chagrin
Fumbled with the gearshift. Out of the brush
Stepped the hunter, bearing a handmade crow-call,
Grinning a snaggled grin.

                    We asked how far
It was to Shiloh, as if we'd stopped to ask.
—He didn't know, he'd never been on through:
And waited, sky-eyed, for us to go.

Driving interminably, whittling the road to nothing,
Finding no thing which bore the mystic name,
We turned around and came back to the highway,
Wondering if the sign had been a decoy

Or if time had toppled all that was addressed
Along that road. Perhaps under the tangle
Of thorny tomorrows will lie the poems which
We pointed to today but never found

Because, like Shiloh, they were in too deep.

SALT

For some reason none of us ran away to sea.
We were not borne or beckoned by the tides.
Forests and farmlands spread vistas in our veins,
But the sea, never the sea.

Our crabby cousins blew away like Kansas
And ended up in odd places doing odd things;
But none of them ever farmed the ocean beds
To compensate for those years of terrible drouth.

Sisters wed lumberjacks and merchants: men
Who only wet their feet in mortgages,
For we were not ruled or reckoned by the tides
Though our salt ran thin as a dull dream by noon does.

Aunts widowed by the wind took inland men
Whose ancestry stopped at the seashore like a wall.
The hinterlands wrapped us in a mythless shell;
We armed ourselves by land.

But this alone does not explain the darkness
Which overtakes us as the day runs out
Like a silken line consumed by the nibbling tide,
Nor the quick look behind us in the dark.

It is not enough any more—if it ever was—
To be set down in the middle of a century
Whose neither end you've seen: or in a land
Or a sky without a shore to tie to.

Now we are running away, if not to sea
At least to *see*, to say, to sense, to sate:
To burn the wall and to emerge again,
Embracing something more than our own selves.

SEASCAPE: AN INTERIOR

From their infrequent letters in startling English
We learn of Pedro's passing: Pedro who
Robusted days between the heavy hills
And the calm bay, Pedro who snaggled words
Like a private joke imperfectly translated
Out of a big heart which now they say
Has broken from its cage like a crazed jackal
And fallen for sustenance.

Because we have been there twice, because we climbed
Those hills when the morning sky was pink with flamingoes
And day dived upon us crying with pelicans,
Because the cool nights have nuzzled us with sleep
And the grey-green edges of bay fog huddled at our fires,
Because we have come with wonder and left with thanks-
    giving,
We cannot think that Pedro, who captained this port,
Died with a hungry heart.

Now what they say of Elena, taken from school
In Arizona, of Jesus on the big farm miles away,
Of Julio trading fish in Hermosillo for a girl's favor,
Of little José whose hard cough racks the grey hush of
   pelicans,
Of Mamacita staunch in the stooped doorway,
Is only secondary: Pedro was the one.

How we came to find them, and to love them,
Must have been as Pedro, washed with shipwreck,
Coming the first time into that placid bay:
The same wonder. The same fulfillment.
The same sure knowledge that nothing falls
Or breaks, or spills, or vanishes, land sea or air.

Now we must write them in our imperfect gringo
That we are coming again, that we are bringing
A few small things for the holidays, that we hope
The fishing will be good, and they are all well.

CONTINGENT

In water as in wind we shape
Our arms around familiar bodies.
Beds know the way we are;
Chairs turn to living shells.

The runner finds earth
First fact of his running;
The medium of the flier
Is air, his coexistent.

Man the Upright is a lie.
Something is always there
To cradle him: water,
Earth, fire, or air.

(On a painting by Everett Spruce)

This sky awaits great things. This spare outcropping
Of mountain presupposes it is earth
In whose whole eye these blessings will reflect:
Lyric and logic met in a wide moment.

Plato on horseback—earth, water, fire and air—
Covers this event from either bank,
For here is total law and perfect vision:
Animal and angel look upon this river.

Here is the wind brushed upon glinting flanks,
Here space suffers no serious confinement
And great things wait to happen, while the eye
Of wisdom watches from the mountainside.

At thirty thousand feet the air
And the comedy run thin. The Texan's bravura
Washes the cabin like ammonia.

A scrim of frozen clouds
Separates us from the wounds of Appalachia;
But Our Hero, his ego wounded afresh
By that shot still echoing through his western world,
Roars like a Lion at his own unwitting feast.

White cloud explodes across the wings as we
Plough in to find a hole to Kennedy.
Under the dark water, darker images:
Clouds? or reefs? or schools of creatures like
Ourselves?

We grind against the air.
Put up or shut up says the hush
Which falls now.
                    The holiday
Is suddenly over. Up there, where our lives
Spun on a silver thread of disbelief,
All that depended on our presence had to wait.
Wine worked, potatoes sprouted in dark places,
Moths blinked as buttons fell from last year's suit,
And our hands were tied.

                    In Manhattan
The Shubert is real, though its folded fantasy
Is stored in Props. Somewhere in the city
The Texan is sweating over a deal gone wrong.

I lie in a dark room wanting to go back.

11

Even in the dark
I know him. My headlights
Feel for him and draw him
Mindless as a moth
Into the car.

He is an old child
Of my own age, but he is
Ravaged by the weathers
Of gossip: how he committed
An act of violence upon a young boy.

His strange eye glints
In the carlight. His tied tongue
Thanks me in torment while we
Survey each other
Looking straight ahead.

Even in the dark
I know him. Through the labyrinth
Of scars I bring the wineskin
To Tantalus;
Will he remember?

It is ourselves we mourn when tides recede
To leave our bleached bones balanced on the ripples
Of sand and foam. We are the only cripples
In evidence; all other things are freed
By ebb and flow. In our insatiable greed
We tied the farmhouse down, the crib, the stables,
The rickrack fence, the doghouse, picnic tables . . .
Even the wind's denied the tethered steed.
So these are our bones, left from other summers.
We grieve among them, choosing what we will
To put ourselves together from the grave;
But the tide departs, erasing half the numbers,
And, uninstructed, we have not the skill
To make us whole with these few parts we have.

I have seen this same poor potted lobster
In a hundred advertisements: he leers gloomily
From the captain's table on the U.S.S. *America,*
Gawks dumbly on the beach at Montauk Point
(You like it, it likes you). There's something
About a lobster that makes no mistake.

Or could it be that this is my mistake?
That something real distinguishes one lobster
From every other one of them, that something
Akin to mankind makes them all stare gloomily
Out of their stalked eyes? Aye, there's a point:
Death in the red is frowned on in America.

All aliens cry *America, America!*
Till tip and tax establish their mistake;
Then they are told it isn't nice to point.
My sympathies are somehow with the lobster
Who, emigrated from his waters gloomily
And promised nothing, immigrates to something.

Maybe our problem is that we want something
Better than anything, in America.
I once saw a blue-lipped Jewess staring gloomily
Into a crepe suzette, and my mistake
Was seeing all Jews in her, as every lobster
Is the one on shipboard or at Montauk Point.

I'm not at all sure I have made my point,
Bedevilled by a philosophic something
Which mixes up mankind in sauce of lobster.
If there's a point, it is that in America
We classify each other—a mistake
Which leaves us living brotherless and gloomily.

I had not meant to speak my speech so gloomily
Nor illustrate it with so gauche a point.
The nebulous moral is no rare mistake.
Go throw your arms around someone or something;
Invite him into the ark that is America;
Go out and call by name your choice of lobster.

Commit yourself not gloomily to something—
And point out always, friend, that in America
We may mistake the King, *but we dig lobster.*

HUNTING, FISHING AND FOREST SCENES

By Currier & Ives ("Good Luck All Around")

Because I have lined my creel with trout, and you
Display a brace of snipe which you have bagged,
And nearby a gentlewoman and her son
Smile on arriving at an eddying pool
And the sun prisms the sky all down the wood,

Does this convince the looker-on
That God's in his heaven and October sweet
When one may see backgrounded in the scene
The fire-red blast and the partridge torn from air?

Our backs are turned: We all are trading tales.
I have a trout to take a hook from, you
Must praise your snipe, the gentlewoman peers
As if to see what father to her son
Will offer supper if she catches none.

Yet one need not tripod nor plumb nor sextant
To know that here is not good luck all around,
For fast beyond the partridge broke in air
Are two vague innocent figures in their shelter
Above the lake. It is a dirty trick.

Not one of all the pampered pastoral pups
Lapping the trout-laden waters at our feet
Has pricked an ear, nor I, nor you,
Nor even that gentle woman's incurious son.

I do not blame such things for happening
Nor their occasional necessity;
It is the *how* that troubles me, the rendering.
I should have caught this moment a moment later
And we should all be laughing through October
Instead of wondering if it would be proper.

Now I rustle the pages of this essential calendar
To see if perhaps in November's frosted field
Two innocent figures lie in a chilling heap
Of broken partridges. But no. A bright red engine
Of the Chattanooga chuffs placidly
Under the green vantages of Lookout Mountain.

MANDATE

It's all right
To do what you must
If you Belong.

Remember Mrs. Rundle
On the 18th green
At Effingham
When a stranger popped
Out of the bushes
Wearing only
A bowler.

"Are you a member?"
She demanded, and
When he said No,
Clouted him over the
Head with a club.

It could happen to you.
Wear something
Besides a hat
To cover such exigencies.

And keep your dues paid up.

Translating summer into another tongue,
The boat lisps through the cold emerald
Water, through the onyx deeps and the crystal riffles,
Spinning late fallen leaves into yellow chapters
And red oak volumes.

The thermal-knit fisherman flicks ice from his line,
Casting and reeling from bank to boat.
Somewhere a bass is lurking; somewhere a jack
Noses a pebbled recollection of the sporting summer.

Here the long fingers of willows write on the water;
Here the log deciphers the cryptic pool;
The wintering river glosses its margins with meaning.
High on a naked hill the symbolic staccato
Of a yellowhammer shatters the frozen hush.

It has been a long time since the last geese flew.
It will be a long time before they fly again.
But this boat moves north, for the river runs that way:
Summer or winter, this river runs north.

And the fingers of the willows write on the water.

Two night fishers were first to hear the cry.
It made their minnows shiver in the tin bucket.

How innocently it had all begun!—
The river tripping on that tongue of sand,
Those granite arches joining eternities;
Even the moon came down in its pleasant way.

Later, they remembered their rods and reels,
The bait untouched, lines bearing little notches
Of river junk, how the water had gone down.

But at the moment they remembered nothing
Except that terrible cry from the white bridge
Until they tensed their ears
Against the incredible moment of the splash.

It was a woman, I think, said one of the fishermen,
And the other, dazed, agreed it was a woman.
Somewhere in the sudden crowd a spark of laughter
Short-circuited against an elbow.

They washed the river down with lantern light:
Colemans and flashlights and floodlamps and headlights.
The river turned into a ribbon of wet sun.

But wives, if they had disappeared, were not
Reported missing. Husbands were let be
By wives who'd had enough of them, anyway.
So the night went by.
Patrol boats putted irreverently through the hours,
Grappling for garbage only, nothing more.
Their lights sliced the mystic fathoms; turtles turned
And looked surprised and went to deeper beds.
One frog laughed grossly, as if he knew.

As the first light of day came up the river,
They found her, naked as a newborn Eve:
A pink manikin with a small putty bosom
And a pocketknife wound that could not be a wound.
Somehow her makeup had all been washed away—
What final infamy!

But laughter failed;
The crowd dispersed. The two night fishermen
Drifted apart and went their separate ways,
Each looking back to ask, but never asking,
Whether the thing was any way less real
Because the body found was less a body?

So they went home, sleepless, thinking, *The phone
Will wake me up; her family will call
To ask me how it happened; what will I say?*

II

Sitting for a Portrait

. . . Though thou retaine of mee
One picture more, yet that will bee,
Being in thine owne heart, from all malice free.

—John Donne

Beloved of bird
If not of man,
Cornelia fed
The downy swans

On Medley Pond
Until they grew
Both plump and fond
Of Cornelia, who

Forewent the snacks
That served so well
To soothe and lax
The little hell

Her office was.
Though she grew thin,
She loved the state the swans
Were in,

And each noon plied
Their appetites
With boiled or fried
Or frozen bites

Until one day
When she fell ill
The swans' dismay
Was loud and shrill;

But she came not
To calm their hunger.
Whereupon
In choicest anger

They flayed their keeper
With their feathers
Good and proper,
Demanding whether

The Lovely Lady
Of the Crumbs
Was gone for good; he
Said she'd come.

And sure enough,
She did. However,
Meantime his huge rough
Hands had severed

Head from body,
One by one,
And dressed himself
As a noble swan;

And when he took her,
White as snow,
Cornelia never
Let him know.

Waiting to wed Ulysses, four-year letterman,
After his odyssey in the Wildoat Wars,
Penelope went sour. Got miserly and weedy.
Wove days of thinning hope and tore them out
Like biting fingernails at a dark window.

He skirted Lotos, blinded Cyclopes,
Encountered Circes with a comely courage,
And sent back clippings from the local press.
Men who had known him marvelled; married ladies
Swooned in Society and pined in privy.

But to gather together after all these years!
Ah, this is the Argus who raises up his head
To sniff us up and down, and that's the nurse
Who knows our scars, on whom we must enjoin
Silence to silence the rattling at our gates.

Now while the punchbowl bleeds with red ice roses
And four hundred babysitters are waiting to collect,
I must confess I'm the world's worst with names:
Are you that poor crone in the tattered shawl?
Am I that weathered god with the slack bow?

FOREWORD FOR A SECOND EDITION

Duned in the doom of his impeccable grave
My uncle never guessed how in demand
Would be his letters from the western land
Where he had gone for his health, that rave on rave
Would squander his unlearned assets of love
For his dear older brother left to read
The anguish in these lines, nor that our greed
Could dig him up, though he were dead enough.
Had this insatiable hunger knocked on doors
Sooner by forty years, if those who throw
Three dollars down for his incredible verse
Had done it earlier, he would on sunlit shores
Live now who died in San Antonio
And came home wreathed in garlands, in a hearse.

A thousand things went wrong when my Grandfather's angels
Deserted him, and he never got them back;
But he barged clumsily ahead, thinking, I suppose,
That if he tried enough things, one would work out.
He witched a dozen wells, and they were dry.
He planted corn; the weevils ate it up.
He courted Jessie, fifty years his junior,
But she caught some contagion she could not lose.
I never knew a man who kept so busy
In face of sure defeat, who persevered
Through blunder after blunder, who declined
To sit and think things out, who had the gall
To reckon the law of averages would revert,
Sooner or later, some victory to him.

Some people said his troubles came about
Simply because he thought the way he did
About the Color Question (in my South
You just don't think that way, but Grandfather did).
Whatever brought it on, there were high haints
In Grandfather's head, and it seemed to me
He'd never shake them. He ran for Constable
And got eight votes (his family gave him four).
His choicest fields grew up in johnson grass.
And two by two the martins left his house.

He did not sulk around; he had a great,
Hopeful, primitive, all-encompassing
Radiance for the people that he knew;
Swapped his best yarns around the country store
And laughed (Lord, how he laughed!), though no one else **did**;
Beat backs, shook hands, grew stooped, got gray,
Shuffled, and drew the fabric of his wedding suit
Closer about his thin chest, going home.

I had learned little of that southern passion
The novelists celebrate: I thought of something else
Whenever I heard the term. But Grandfather had it,
And it was too big for any man to house.
He finally broke, like a keg of elderberry wine,
Riding the back seat of a Greyhound bus
(Going to Birmingham, they said he said),
And two bucks bore him home, light as a willow.
Stay a spell, we said, but they declined,
Going like darkest angels in the night,
Taking at last his surest victory.

I was just playing
With the dog, baying
As a boy will,
When he turned tail
And let out a wail
And ran over the hill.

Then I on all fours
Went to my chores,
And never got up.
My family sighed
And reckoned that I'd
Turned to a pup.

But, child to some other
Than my own mother
And my own sire,
I howled about lunar
Disturbances sooner
Than lack of fire

When I was left
Cold and bereft
Outside at night;
And, gnawing a bone
In time of alone,
Considered my plight.

Then the dog came back
One night with a pack
Of wolves, six or eight;

And I knew my time
Was long past its prime
For playing it straight.

Thus my liaison
Carried them on—
Dead into danger . . .
Out of the cold,
Into the fold,
The trap, the manger.

Then a quick bullet
Skittered the pullet
And murdered one duck
Before the wolves lay
Dead in the hay.
Such was my luck

That father or mother
Stayed the other,
Withheld their fire;
Something, they said
Later, they read
Of my desire . . .

And as they led
Each other to bed,
They left ajar
The door, and I
Crept in, to lie
With the bone of a star.

Of all involvements of the horse with art
Crivelli's S. *George and the Dragon* was
Her favorite. Whenever she got to Boston
To see it, she would whisper "Look at that sneer!
He hates the dragon! Look at that wild eye!"

She said of the damsel kneeling on the rock
"Look at that poor granny in the background
Praying for his deliverance!"

Like George's candy-striped lance, we
Invariably broke up. Had to be hushed
By an attendant. But Granny never noticed;
She was involved, man. And still is.
Look at that sneer.

     She hates this dragon.

AT THE MUSEUM AGAIN

Fashion be hanged, he said, the dinosaurs
Seemed much too thin this year; they rattled about
With bow legs bared. This philosophical look
Disquieted him. He thought, with Rabelais,
What a sad end it is when one is buried
With a tall erection, wondering about life.

It was ten tedious years since he had been
(A visitor) to the Museum of Natural History.
He had been giddy as the blind goose he was,
Strayed in from the bayou country of the Lowlands,
Poking anatomical slights at outmoded creatures
Whose centuries were rodded up for ridicule.

But then he had not imagined how extinct
One can become in a decade, nor how the world ends
Somewhere somehow with every turn of second;
That, coming again, the terrible juveniles
From P.S. 28 would look on his contemplating
With puzzlement, and whisper among themselves
That he *belonged* here, a part of the exhibit.

Obligingly beneath their curious eyes
He turned to stone; and an attendant came
To hang a temporary tag on him
Until he could be classified and placed
In the catalogue, along with his own kind.

In the ring, under the lights,
He moves like a fine machine well oiled.
His muscles throb with applause.
His eyes smoulder like astonished dragons.

At home he is a grandfather:
Bumbling and gentle, haunted by the stillness,
Foolish upon the old woman maybe
Twice a month; there are no dragons there.

He will not bring her to the arena.
She sits with the children's children,
Annoying them at TV: *I'll bet your Grand*
Has thrown The Great Bolo out of the ring by now.

And he, but half conscious of his loneliness
In this beautiful aura,
Remembers himself at twenty:
Changeless for all time.

Addicted to the symbolists of youth
We share that dream, distressed to find
Ourselves outraged by his impermanence.
We shriek for his downfall, and we all fall down.

What we already know diminishes you
Who know not even the movement of light
Curled like a blind kitten in your dacron straw.
What we already know about the world
Presupposes what we know of you
But of ourselves we are diminished by.

You deserve Kings! Take grandmothers instead:
One with a migraine bolted to her head,
The other too good for pain. Take grandfathers:
Old gamblers at the checkerboard of days,
Swinging the frankincense of gnarled briars,
Grunting, contented that the Lord
Has come to save them of their Sunday sins.

You are already hundredly magnified
By what we know: now you are born
In evergreen concern, now you begin to die,
Stars of gingerbread over your threatened brow,
Magnificent blindness: crosses for us all.

At four, among his Sunday aunts and uncles,
He swashed verbatim through Red Riding Hood
With such authority that we were sure
We saw the bad wolf racing down the wood.

At ten, he ignored the shame attending ruffles
And pantaloons and the sissy finger sign
And the raw giggles, and gave us pure
Convincing Barrie, and never muffed a line.

Then on a narrow stage amid the rest
Of Shakespeare's teen-age cast, he was the wild
And restless Dane . . . but it was not his test;
It was ours. We could not find our child.

Now all those kin are dead, or somehow gone,
Or indisposed by their infirmities,
And seldom write to ask of him, or phone;
And we volunteer nothing, knowing less

Of his privation in the bouldered city
Since the door opened out and he stepped down
Into a sunset like footlights. He rejected pity
When he took that crown.

But we look everywhere for that austere face,
Hoping whatever world he would attain
Will take that strangeness with the public praise
The arena of our love could not contain.

We never knew when next the fox might strike,
But many a dark night lying in the loft
Straining our ears to catch the swift, the soft,
The cunning coming of him or his like,
We held a fortress as men hold a wake:
Silent and grim, bound to a solemn task
Which wasn't interrupted even to ask
The time; our boyhood honor was at stake.
And often when the cock crew, shaking fire
Out of the morning and the misty mow,
We stayed on, staring, hard put to leave off,
Lest in the wood the image of desire
Spring up behind us yapping, although now
We know we've kept this vigil long enough.

Their father, hoping to be left alone
To wade the tules for a catch of bream,
Loaded them on the raft and pushed it out.
Tumbled from grace, they burned and yelled
Until from the depths there surfaced suddenly
A turtle crusty as a pirate's cache,
Barnacled with bloodstone and marigold.

A sign! whispered the forsaken sister,
As though the Son Himself had traced a fish
In Galilean sand. With a sodden rope
She lassoed the creature, who obligingly
Towed them toward the tules.
                       In
His phosphorous wake she rode like Venus,
Turning to her bug-eyed little brother
A quaintly righteous smile, pale at the edges.

Their father, dangling one drowning bream like an amulet,
Waded ashore where the monster lumbered out;
But as soon as the sun struck the mossy
Hexagons of its shell, the thing disintegrated—
And the father, with uplifted oar to smash it,
Felt his muscles take the shock.

                          They kept
The moral (if any) to themselves, wisely
Pretending it was an everyday affair.
Even the bream fanning the golden air of the tules
Kept their mouths shut, as they discovered.

Once as I clung
To the arm of my father
I hung
In the water.

How deep was too deep
I could not fathom:
His white legs kept
An easy rhythm.

Then down to my chin
And up from my doubt
He let me in,
He let me out.

And when at length
He let me free
I swam with strength
Of two or three.

But he went down
All green and gold.
I watched him drown.
And then grow old.

My Aunt Rebecca, stiff as a Baptist poker,
Let all those Algerians perish like cockroaches
Inside her radio, and never sent to CARE.

Her eyes took on a grim, avenging glint
Whenever those Catholics in Italy
Were damned by being undammed in their beds.

But Aunt Rebecca clucked like Lady God
On August days when clouds biled up from West:
She henned even little dark Protestants out of the weather.

No matter what brawny field hand got belled in
(She didn't cotton to insurance companies),
It was Rebecca held the cellar door.

When they were all inside her earthen bosom
Coughing and sweating, Aunt Rebecca sang
A hymn or two, which outdid any storm;

And little Protestants giggled in the dark,
Hounds bayed while treeing visions of the wild,
And grown folks called "Amen!" to drown her out.

How many more she might have saved from wind
Or hail or lightning, we will never know.
An elderberry sprang up on the shelter

Whose roots thrust downward through geography,
Theology, Rebecca in the dark,
And wine distilled from her old righteous bones.

ABOUT GRAMPA, WHO DIED POOR

My grandfather in his once-Spencerian hand
Cribbed by the cold which scotched his ancient bones
Wrote two-cent postcards out of Dixieland
To twenty kin and near-kin, Smith and Jones
And several mixed up of a foreign name,
Saying *Now I am free, I might arrange a trip* . . .
Ready to travel before the postman came:
Clothes in a parcel, medicines in a grip.
But those who answered said they had the flu,
Or were about to move, or *Maybe later;*
And he, having nothing, nothing whatever to do,
Got too old even for the elevator,
Much less the train—lamenting most, no doubt,
The forty cents it took to feel them out.

III

For All That Is

For all that is, is lonely; all that may
Will be as lonely as is that you see;
The lonely heart sings on a lonely spray,
The lonely soul swings lonely in the sea,
And all that loneliness is beautiful.

—*James Stephens*

r what the causes were
history's impersonal tide,
madness and the stir
hearts when headlines opened wide
say that on July
d, in nineteen fifty-nine,
Or so   late, a man whom you and I
Knew well, tell, or was felled; and we knew why.
But in the course of days we sleep, we dine,
We catch the bus for work. Injustices
Are daily bread; and we forget his face.
We wonder, sometimes, where (or if) he is;
And tell each other, There, but for the grace . . .

And wake up knowing he is in this place.

June, and my innocence dies,
My young pride crumbles.
There is lightning in my pocket,
A wreath around my past.

The air I displaced in April
Wraps me like a shroud.
I am the echo
Of a candle burning.

When I rode into manhood
I fell from my white horse;
Now I walk backwards
Carrying a donkey.

The wind blows through
The shattered wing.
My love is such a
Foreign thing

I cannot see her
Face. I try.
There is a bandage
On the sky.

But I remember
How her tears
Welled up against
The dam of years.

My heart is honey.
Are you sure
It is manly
To endure?

When I was the child in the belly of the bone
And the wine in the apple came out of the stone,
Then the bees laid gold from the heath to the house
And the sheep-girls sang Carouse! carouse!

The well, which came up cold and clear,
Hosted suddenly two tame deer,
While doves with greenery in their bills
Strung garlands over the stricken hills.

When I was a child with eyes like wings
And the fenceposts turned to living things
And the world was whole as the world she gave,
They laid my mother in the grave.

Then the sun came down and the stars came down
And the great sky knelt for a moment down,
And she was the child and I was grown—
And the wine in the apple came out of the stone.

I have dwelt wholly
Nor even partly
Fringed by the squally
Suburbs, the smartly
Stereolized set.
I have kept warily
To my brown cave
Narrowly, narrowly
Like a grave,
But never To Let.

On a mild March day
In the wide streets
Children, like washday
Lines the eye meets,
Flap and fret.
My heart is a hermit
Coiled in its earth;
Akin to the worm, it
Breeds in its berth—
Childless yet.

Mothers at five
Stop screaming; primp.
The kids, alive
(Surprised), skimp
Water and soap.
Father will come
Coated and checked
And crowned at home
By his own respect,
Lean with hope.

Break be his body,
Drink be his blood;
Be his name Daddy,
Better be stud.
We all need shoes.
Thus do nameless
Clerks disappear
Into all aimless
Seasons of year
And never make news.

Christ be hung
Each Monday week
Where wire is strung
From a pole to the peak
Of a G.I. loan.
Better, I think,
My narrow cave
And a little drink
Than to know they gave
Their flesh this stone.

AT THE COUNTY FAIR

Armed with some merciless notions, the high school band
Ambushed Sousa outside the poultry building,
Seeing, as it were, the whites of the eyes
Of twenty village queens in pastel formals,
Each with her pastel heart set on the crown:
Miss Benton County Fair of 1960.

In the pigeon cages, a general rout ensued.
The pouters pouted, the fantails fanned, the
Trumpeters trumpeted loud and long.
The nuns and helmets claimed immunity
By their vestures, and what's more:
The archangels wondered who in hell
Had stolen their thunder and jumped Judgment Day.
The English carriers carried on, if not in English;
The racing homers would have raced home gladly
Except for U. S. Steel which does a prison make.
The tumblers tumbled. A magpie croaked Retreat.

Shall I report that the new queen fell on her face?
That the M.C. was exiled for certain unmanly remarks?
That a child of six picked the locks on the pigeon cages—
Or the band, forty strong in brand-new uniforms,
Fell into a chasm which opened miraculously?

No; but a moment later the C of C
Manager was seen to snap an old lady's head off,
And, wondrous to tell, her body was borne up
By two white sacred doves who through it all
Had kept their peace, though they had won
Nothing at all, not even a white ribbon.

At twenty-one
I was pursued
By a wall of flame
In a scarlet wood;

But I escaped.
Now I inquire
At every door
"A little fire?"

WILD CHIVES

Christmas, 1966

I

Here where November was, December is,
And the white angel leans as if to find
Among the leaves a hand which once was his,
Holding a rose, an April in his blind

Eyes. Whatever was too mortal for this place
Disintegrates beneath the dunes of time.
That light which shined so brightly on his face
Is caught in the stone of his angelic mime.

But, born beyond the fence of history,
The wild chives lift their crowns, halos of stars;
And the white angel, uprooted by the tree,
Stares past the wall and will, and sees our wars.

II

Gentle as starlight, snow begins to fall . . .
The season's first, eloquent and benign.
Looking to what's at hand—the flake, the wall,
The chives—we push the other out of mind.

The hungry birds to our beneficence
Come trusting as a lamb, or dumb as ox,
Asking no questions. They know the difference
Between a full heart and an empty box.

52

And even the angel, careless with his limb,
Offers some refuge and a little food;
For man, who has dominion over him,
Is (at this season especially) rich and good.

So we hang blessings and they are consumed.
We give, that we be given in return:
The scriptures sanction it. But the snow has tombed
The angel, and our candles will not burn.

III

Out there, beyond the moment, past the wall
Buried like a conscience, past the edge
Of land and sea, the dark of death is all
We give and get. It is the iron wedge

We drive between ourselves this Christmas Day.
Separate from each other in our cells
Of singularity, we cannot weigh
The terrible price of what the other sells.

We sit in tinselled folly, making song
As empty as the platter has become,
While somewhere out beyond the white and long
Stretches of space our guilts lie deep and dumb.

Christ Jesus has delivered the daily news.
Make haste to hide it lest the children see
And learn too soon how badly we abuse
Each other from the manger to the tree.

IV

Under the snow the angel seeks his hand.
The birds seek shelter in their own grey down.
The wild chives, shaken by the day's demand,
Still hold aloft one single perfect crown.

How doubt undoes a man is what the thing
Concerns itself with mostly. Orpheus
Gave up Eurydice to doubt. Lot left
His wife consumed by it to salt the plain
Outside of Sodom. When we tune ourselves
To homing stars, we wonder if perhaps
The enemy's rocket shares the same platform,
If we shall be blown up instead of guided
Naturally (or divinely) to our own doors.

So we unravel: seek consolation
In dark places, darkly manipulating
Ourselves or strangers, crying out for comfort.
We who hardly dared peruse the Personals
Out of a nameless guilt now make the front page:
Stare dumbly at the beast who bears our name.

Doubt is the blood that renews us night by night
And is our merciless punishment by day:
To bow our heads so low we cannot see
That fire, the immaculate thievery of stars.

EPITHALAMION

I lie beside my Mary lamb
(My Mary lies asleep)
And all I ever was or am
Is twice as tall and deep.

I walked in woods, I strolled by streams;
They towered, or they hurried;
But something circled in my dreams
Unnamed before I married.

I lie beside my Mary lamb;
Lamb-like my Mary lies
And creates in me all I am
In her hushed eyes.

First the bird, and now the cat.
All domesticity ends in grief:
The bride in her bower to her ultimate bier,
The groom in whose groin pride was fat
Falls on himself in disbelief,
The child in the womb chokes in the gear
That somehow failed. First the bird,
And now the cat. It is not fair
That one so handsomely endowed
Should go so young. But, as the Word
Was to begin with, it is (spare,
Hurt, dismayed) now, over the shroud.
Wounds we may weather, pain allay,
Triumph we can tell the press of.
Grief knows no mercy such as that.
Say on—but how little we can say!
Stranger, we learn to mention less of
First the bird, and now the cat.

Out of the darkness the voice of my mother, dead
So long now I cannot think about her face,
Says "Hello, son"—and I, too dazed for reason,
Reply hello. She asks if I am well,
And I say yes, reasonably so; the bad leg
Is kicking up a little. (She does not laugh.)
And what have I been doing? . . . A few poems,
An essay now and then to keep the wolf away;
Praying for a publisher ("I pray a lot these days").

There is a wary hush along the wire.
She asks uneasily, "You haven't left
The ministry, have you, son? Poems and essays
Sound like such hungry things to do."

Well, yes, but you get used to hunger. What
Was that about the ministry? "You're not
Abandoning it? Your father was so keen
To have you follow in his footsteps."

Not mine. For a moment, yes.
Now I am crushed by light. Whoever she was
When she called, she is not now;
And I am someone else: No, I tell her gently,
I will never give up this rich life
Of ministering to people's needs, Mother.

"I'm so happy to hear you say that.
I knew you'd change. Leave those hungry things
To people with dirty minds. Remember,
Cleanliness is next to godliness. Goodbye."

What terrible news to burden someone with!
All I can think of as I hang up the phone
Is whether she called Collect. I think she did.

It is a gaunt grey day of slim promise:
From rut to roof the skiffed air hangs ice.
Sparrows, fluffed in their feathered selves,
Blow about their small ragged businesses.
The fox keeps his own hungry counsel in the hill.
The cows turn their crusted haunches to the wind.

I in the fire-flaked window harbor guilt:
Involved in this natural history
Of man and beast, I contemplate what chores
I might devise to ease an elemental cruelty,
What pains I have taken to house myself
Against the siege, how little I have done
To domicile that innocence outside.

Gloss February's daybook with a lie:
Slogged forth to feed the wild and blanket tame,
But did not mind the cold—was warm inside.

Our forte is guilt diminished by comparison:
The neighbors, too, have not stirred out all day.
Night spreads across this uncommitted country
As easy as the ending of the world.

COUNTRY STORE

Here is no crystalline and chrome
Superdrome
Dispensing tinned and instant Home;
Here is no slavishly split-level fare
Of frozen joy or cellophaned despair—
Here, in a high diagonal of bright air,
Is our own dust, or dust that was our fathers
(And some others)
Which no one ever bothers
Any more. There is a pleasant
Wit and wisdom present
Which the late hour doesn't
Diminish at all, but intensifies
Until the tales, the gossip, and the outright lies
Wrap us in our own legend, like the flies
Webbed in high corners. Time is a patient bride
Who waits for each of us somewhere outside
Until the sun goes greening down the wide
Familiar hill to chores,
Until we settle Washington and the wars,
And say goodbye at last, and close the doors.

CAMP MEETING

Here spread a feast of Christian grace
Of chicken grease and johnson grass
Of sermons fleshed by dance and drink
And Satan at the rinky-tink.

Peace garbs itself in holy dress
Of fire and brimstone zealousness
Of ladies who get saved in tongues
And men who jeopardize their lungs.

Here boogey men are born to boo
At children nights the whole week through
But exorcised by all the jar
The devil watches from afar.

Babes take their milk from mothers who're
Big on the bridegroom of the poor
While God disguised in a glint of steel
From summer's belfry starts to peal.

The table laden end to end
Weds hungry foe to hungry friend
Somewhere between baked beans and tea
Swallowed by eternity.

At the Fair Again

Hushed in their midnight stanchions the cows browse
In dreams of summer pastures, ill at ease
Beneath the ribbons their good natures won.

Across the mucky midway, in a cage
With a golden pheasant and his wife,
A spotted fawn, an accidental display,
Nibbles the beargrass as he walks the fence.

Old ladies with poems in their grotesque bags,
With surgery fluent as silver on their tongues,
Tripped oh-ing from the arts and flowers building
To feed the fawn gay nibbles of their fingers;
Men sized him up; kids fell upon their knees.

Someone who knows (thus we are all informed)
Said that the county agent brought him in,
That wound or weather felled him. Nursed to health
By 20,000 eyes, how shall he be
Wild enough ever to go fully free?

The cows in their stanchions know the time of chores.
The pheasants, born to fences, seek no doors.
But the fawn goes back and forth
While the watchman snores.

Suddenly the world depends on you. The wall
Hangs from your picture holding its breath
As if, were your likeness moved, it might fall
Upon the air and the useless floor beneath.
Waking, the day awaits to hear the tick
Of you before continuing its rise.
All that was dead is suddenly somehow quick
To stir: dogs, milk trucks, and other liberties.
And I, dying all night lest you be gone
In dream or real with some dark charioteer
When I should wake, myself leap up like dawn
To feel you stirring—oh alive! alive!

All things assume their native postures. I've
Been reprieved, thank God!—and you're still here.

ABOUT THE AUTHOR

EDSEL FORD is a native of Alabama, but he spent most of his youth in Arkansas, where he now lives. He served in the United States Army for two years after receiving the Bachelor of Arts degree (1952) from the University of Arkansas, to which he returned in 1966 to accept the University's Distinguished Alumnus Citation.

Most of the poems in this collection have previously been published in a wide range of periodicals. Other collections, now out of print, were published in 1956: *The Manchild from Sunday Creek;* in 1961: *A Thicket of Sky;* and in 1965: *Love Is the House It Lives In.*

Mr. Ford served on the Governor's Advisory Committee for the Arts and Humanities in Arkansas 1966–1967. His poetry has been recognized by a number of awards in addition to the Devins Award, among which are four from The Poetry Society of America, in 1962, 1964, 1966, and 1967. Ten of the poems in *Looking for Shiloh* have been recorded by their author for the National Archives, at the invitation of The Library of Congress.